STATE TREES

Newly Revised Edition

written and illustrated by

Olive L. Earle

William Morrow and Company
New York 1973

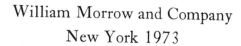

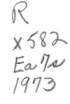

INDEX

Printed in the United States of America.
Library of Congress Catalog Card Number 73-4932
ISBN 0-688-30083-9 (lib. bdg.)
1 2 3 4 5 77 76 75 74 73

Sunlight and rainwater, air and soil—a tree is made from these. They are the magic ingredients that transform a tiny seed into the mightiest tree. Sometimes trees of the same species may differ in their shape or in the height reached at maturity. And leaves on a very young tree are apt to be larger than those on an older one.

Man uses trees in countless ways, from eating their fruits to using their wood to build his home or to make his musical instruments, baseball bats, paper, and cellophane.

One of the truly important benefits received from trees is the beauty they bring to our lives. Most people have a favorite tree, and now all the states have chosen a special one as a symbol. In many cases children's votes decided which tree should be the State Tree.

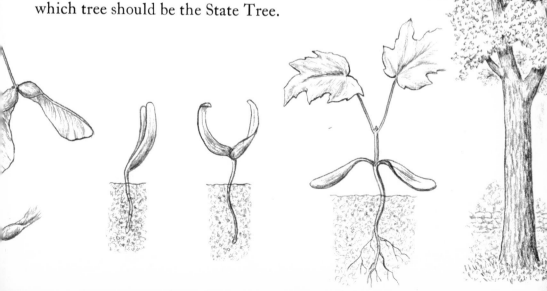

(Paper birch, canoe birch, silver birch)

This tree flourishes best in the moist soil beside a river or lake, where it may grow to a height of seventy feet. Always at home in a cold climate, it grows on mountain heights, though as a much smaller tree. It is even found as far north as the Arctic Circle, but there it is a dwarf only about six inches in height.

The white birch is also called the paper birch, because the chalk-white bark can be peeled off in thin paperlike layers. Loss of bark, peeled off by thoughtless campers, results in a tree's going through life scarred, for the bark does not renew itself. If layers of the bark are removed and the injury girdles the tree, it dies because the food channels are destroyed.

The name *canoe birch* comes from one of the many uses to which the Indians put this tree. A framework with a tough sheath of waterproof birch bark made a canoe which, though light, could carry a man on the roughest water.

The triangular leaves have notched margins. The erect catkins of the tiny female flowers are shorter

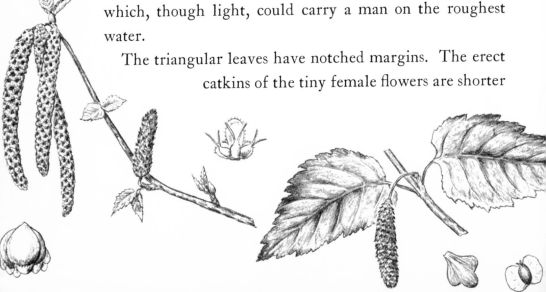

than the pendent, pollen-bearing male
tassels, which may be four inches long.
Formed the previous year, the catkins grow
near each other on the same little branch.
When ripe, the tiny winged seeds are scat-
tered by the wind.

Birchwood is highly valued and is used
for many things—from spools (for thread)
to furniture.

Another variety of birch, originally from
northern Europe, is also called white birch.
Often planted in parks and gardens, this
white-barked tree has drooping branches,
unlike the American tree, whose branches
point upward.

(Ohio buckeye, fetid buckeye, stinking buckeye)

This member of the buckeye group rarely grows taller than fifty feet. It is known as the fetid, or stinking buckeye because of the unpleasant odor of its bitter sap.

In many ways this tree is similar to its Old World relative, the horse chestnut. Both have a compound leaf made up of several leaflets radiating from the tip of a long stalk. The horse chestnut has seven leaflets, while the buckeye usually has five, from four to six inches long. Both trees have one or two large shiny seeds enclosed in a prickly husk, which splits when the fruit, or nut, is ripe. Long ago, it is said, this brown nut was compared to the eye of a buck and so gave the tree its name.

The greenish-yellow flowers grow in a loosely branched cluster called a panicle. Some of them have pollen, and others have the seed-bearing ovary.

Because the wood of the buckeye is very light and does not split readily, it is used in luggage and for making toys. It was much in demand for making artificial limbs before lightweight metals came into general use.

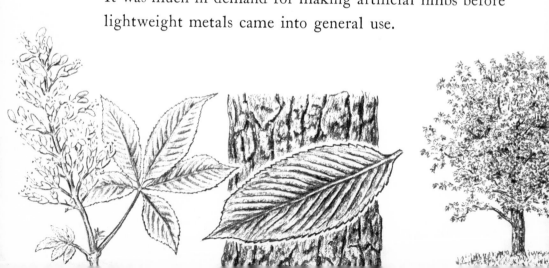

In the spring, flowering dogwood in bloom looks like a new snowdrift and is recognized easily. But the actual yellow-green flowers are seldom noticed. Tiny and inconspicuous, about twenty of them grow in a flat cluster at the center of four broad bracts, or leaflets, which often are mistaken for the petals of a white flower. By autumn, each flower may have formed an oval scarlet seed-bearing berry; usually, only a few of these seeds develop. Many birds like the fruit and help to scatter the seed.

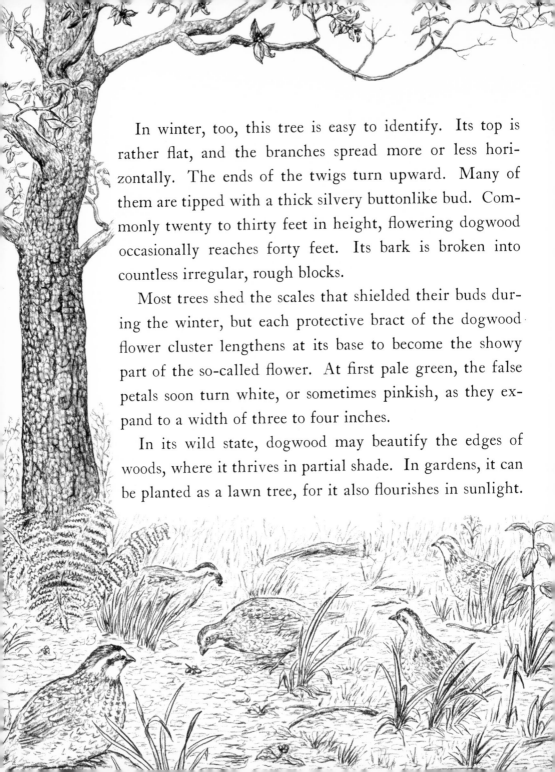

In winter, too, this tree is easy to identify. Its top is rather flat, and the branches spread more or less horizontally. The ends of the twigs turn upward. Many of them are tipped with a thick silvery buttonlike bud. Commonly twenty to thirty feet in height, flowering dogwood occasionally reaches forty feet. Its bark is broken into countless irregular, rough blocks.

Most trees shed the scales that shielded their buds during the winter, but each protective bract of the dogwood flower cluster lengthens at its base to become the showy part of the so-called flower. At first pale green, the false petals soon turn white, or sometimes pinkish, as they expand to a width of three to four inches.

In its wild state, dogwood may beautify the edges of woods, where it thrives in partial shade. In gardens, it can be planted as a lawn tree, for it also flourishes in sunlight.

(Red fir, Oregon pine, Oregon spruce)

Often used as a Christmas tree, a young Douglas fir, with its lowest branches sweeping the ground, is shaped like a pyramid. Older Douglas firs have straight reddish-brown trunks bare of branches for about one third of their height. A mature tree is likely to be two hundred feet tall with a trunk six feet across. Occasionally one of these trees may live for a thousand years and grow to a height of more than three hundred feet—almost as tall as a huge redwood. Having grown rapidly when young, such a giant Douglas fir would not be nearly as old as the redwood.

The Douglas fir differs from true firs in various ways. For one thing, its cones hang down, like those of the spruce and the pine. True firs have erect cones that shed their scales by degrees. The Douglas fir drops its cones whole when they ripen in the autumn. They are peculiar cones,

with long three-pronged tongues sticking out between the thin scales. Two winged seeds are at the base of each scale. Each two- to four-inch cone develops from a cluster of reddish flowers which bloom, in spring, near the ends of the branches. The bright-red pollen-bearing male flowers grow in separate groups.

The soft flattened inch-long needles grow thickly in spirals around the twigs. A needle stays on the tree from three to five years; new growth keeps the tree evergreen.

Growing in dense forests, this towering tree is one of the most useful of all trees. The lumber is used wherever strength is needed, as in masts, railroad ties, and buildings. No part of a cut tree is wasted.

The American elm is often planted along streets. It grows wild in woods and fields. When it is not crowded by other trees, the ridged, gray-barked trunk divides at a point ten or twenty feet above the ground. The boughs arch outward, and each bough has drooping branches that end in a lacework of reddish twigs. This typical fountain pattern is not always followed, for an elm may have wide-spread, almost angular limbs. And when growing in woods, the main trunk may not divide to form a wide crown for perhaps fifty feet. Records show that the elm

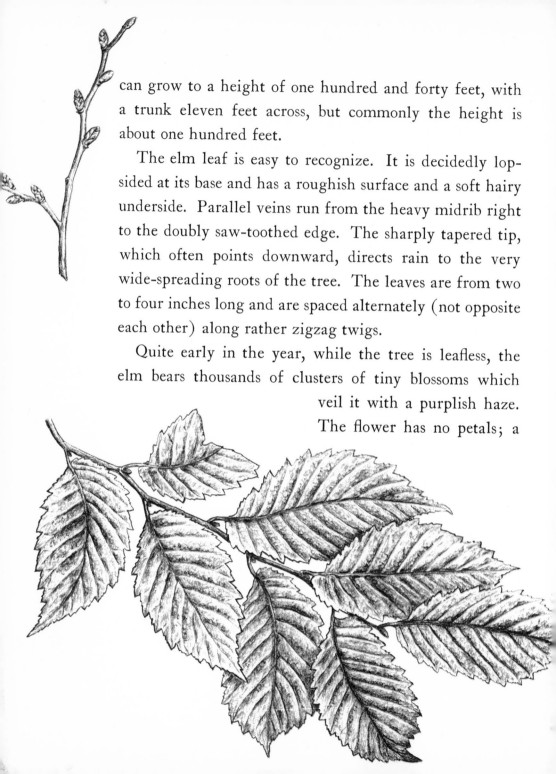

can grow to a height of one hundred and forty feet, with a trunk eleven feet across, but commonly the height is about one hundred feet.

The elm leaf is easy to recognize. It is decidedly lop-sided at its base and has a roughish surface and a soft hairy underside. Parallel veins run from the heavy midrib right to the doubly saw-toothed edge. The sharply tapered tip, which often points downward, directs rain to the very wide-spreading roots of the tree. The leaves are from two to four inches long and are spaced alternately (not opposite each other) along rather zigzag twigs.

Quite early in the year, while the tree is leafless, the elm bears thousands of clusters of tiny blossoms which veil it with a purplish haze. The flower has no petals; a scalloped cup contains the seed-bearing ovary and from four to nine pollen-bearing stamens that hang from it like a little fringe. The elm differs from many other hardwood trees, for most of them have the stamens in one flower and the ovary in another.

The seed rapidly develops into a little winged fruit; its oval papery covering is flat, notched at the tip, and slightly hairy. The ripe seed sails away on the wind, and if it settles in just the right spot and escapes being eaten by a bird, soon takes root.

The tough yellowish-brown wood is difficult to split and is used for making furniture and many other things.

This beautiful tree has terrible enemies. One kind of beetle and its larvae chew and destroy the leaves, and a worse variety penetrates the bark, carrying with it a fungus disease that kills the tree.

In the winter, the hemlock's graceful drooping boughs bend, but seldom break, under the weight of heavy snow. In the spring, the somber green foliage is lit by bright new growth. The tiny pale-yellow male flowers and the pinkish-lavender female flowers also appear; they are in separate groups. Later the female flowers will turn into hanging red-brown cones no more than three quarters of an inch long. Two tiny seeds lie under every fertile scale and each is fitted with a transparent wing for use as a sail.

The leaves, or needles, which are about half an inch long, grow in flat sprays and are usually blunt-tipped. Each needle is attached to the slender twig by a threadlike stalk. After three years on the tree, the needle falls, but the base of the woody stalk remains on the twig. The needles, growing in rows, seem to be set only on the sides of the twig, but there are also small upside-down needles on the top of the twig. Two parallel white lines on the underside of the needle contain the microscopic mouthlike openings, called stomata, which all leaves need for the com-

plicated work of producing food material for the tree.

In former years, nothing but the hemlock's bark was utilized by man; it contains tannin, which is used in converting hides into leather. Nowadays the lumber is valued too. It has a special power of gripping nails driven into it. The bark is broadly ridged and may be three inches thick on a mature tree. Such a tree may reach a height of one hundred and sixty feet and might be six hundred years old. The usual height of the eastern hemlock is about one hundred feet.

The western hemlock, which is at home in cool areas where the rainfall is heavy, grows to an even greater height than the eastern hemlock, and its trunk may be as much as ten feet across. The two trees have similar flowering habits, but the cones of the western hemlock are often considerably larger, and usually more pointed.

The spray of needles is not as flat as it is in the eastern species, and each needle's tip is definitely rounded. The markings on the underside are less pronounced.

The western hemlock's bark contains tannin, and its valuable lumber is used for many purposes. As pulpwood, a great deal of it goes into the making of newsprint.

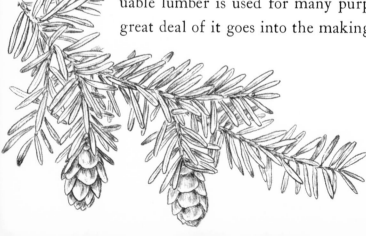

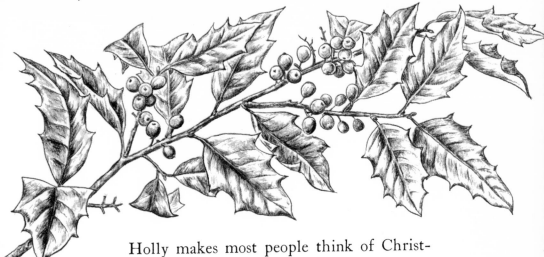

Holly makes most people think of Christmas, when its shiny leaves and scarlet berries make it a favorite decoration. As a result, American holly has been cut so ruthlessly that it has almost disappeared from places where it once grew freely. Now both American and English holly (less hardy, but with bigger berries) are being grown just to provide Christmas greenery. Both kinds are also planted in gardens.

In areas where the winter is cold, holly is a shrub. Farther south, it grows like a tall pyramid, perhaps forty feet high. Occasionally, in an ideal situation, it reaches eighty feet. This gray-barked tree, with its rather short, drooping branches, grows best in rich, moist soil. It is

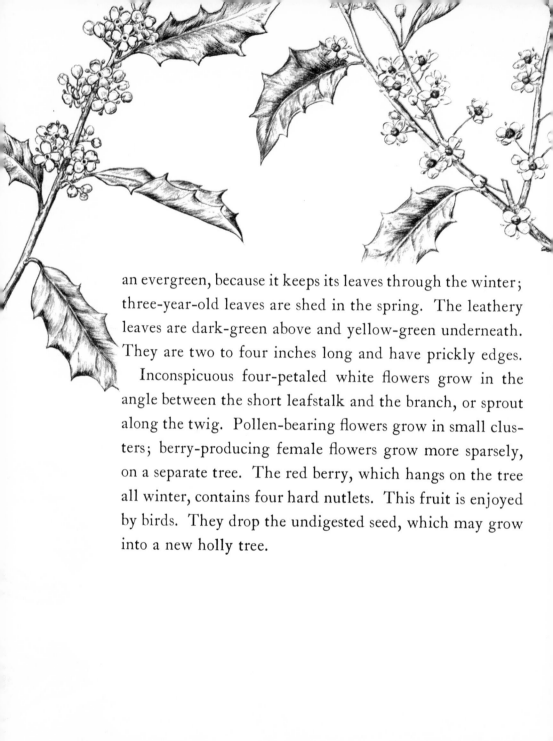

an evergreen, because it keeps its leaves through the winter; three-year-old leaves are shed in the spring. The leathery leaves are dark-green above and yellow-green underneath. They are two to four inches long and have prickly edges.

Inconspicuous four-petaled white flowers grow in the angle between the short leafstalk and the branch, or sprout along the twig. Pollen-bearing flowers grow in small clusters; berry-producing female flowers grow more sparsely, on a separate tree. The red berry, which hangs on the tree all winter, contains four hard nutlets. This fruit is enjoyed by birds. They drop the undigested seed, which may grow into a new holly tree.

This tree, the grandest of the native magnolias, is clothed so thickly in large leathery leaves that it sometimes looks as if it had no trunk or branches. It is an evergreen, for in the spring new leaves are sprouting as the old ones fall. Each young leaf's pale, downy underside soon becomes rust-colored, and its surface takes on a polished dark green.

During the entire summer many fragrant waxen flowers bloom on the stiff upbending twigs. They measure eight or more inches across and have six to twelve creamy petals. The three sepals expand and look like petals. At a purple spot in the center, many stamens and a group of pistils grow. When the seed capsules are ripe, each brownish pod splits, releasing one or two coral-red seeds which dangle awhile by a slender thread.

A fully grown tree is about eighty feet tall, an unusually big one over one hundred feet. The gray-brown trunk may be four feet across. This southern tree grows wild in moist areas, but is also widely cultivated.

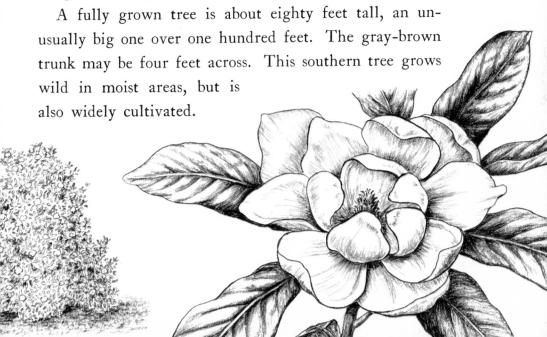

(Swamp maple, scarlet maple)

The maple is Rhode Island's state symbol, with the red maple the favorite species. All year it justifies its name. In winter, the twigs and bud are red. Then, very early in spring, the leafless tree is covered with clusters of tiny red-petaled flowers having either stamens or pistils. Clusters of male or female flowers grow on the same tree or on separate ones. As the young red leaves are turning green, the seeds are ripening.

The joined twin seeds, each with a red wing, are called keys, or (by botanists) samaras. These soon fall and are

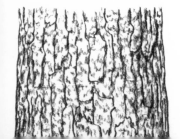

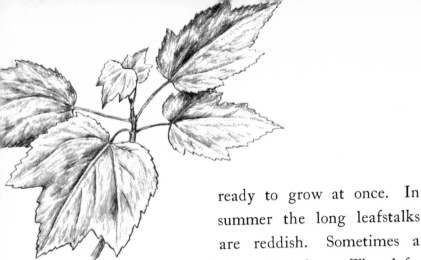

ready to grow at once. In summer the long leafstalks are reddish. Sometimes a leaf has five lobes instead of the typical three. The clefts between them are V-shaped, and their margins are notched irregularly.

The days get shorter and the nights colder. The foliage turns scarlet, for the minute cells of chlorophyll (a Greek word meaning *green leaf*) have broken down and have not been renewed. Now, with the green gone, hidden red and yellow pigments have a chance to show in the display of autumn color. The worn-out leaf falls. The "food factory" shuts down and the tree is ready for the time when its roots will get little or no nourishment from the soil.

The trunk of an old red maple, sixty to ninety feet in height, has a dark-gray bark, ridged and shaggy; its upright branches are paler, and smooth, as the trunk was in youth.

(Hard, or rock maple)   WEST VIRGINIA, WISCONSIN

Indians taught the early settlers how to tap the maple tree for its sweet sap. Modern methods are used now, but the sugar maple tree is still the main source of the famous syrup and sugar. In late winter and very early spring, before the tree's buds swell, sap begins to flow through the tree. The sap is collected by means of a spout driven into the trunk, and then boiled down to syrup and sugar.

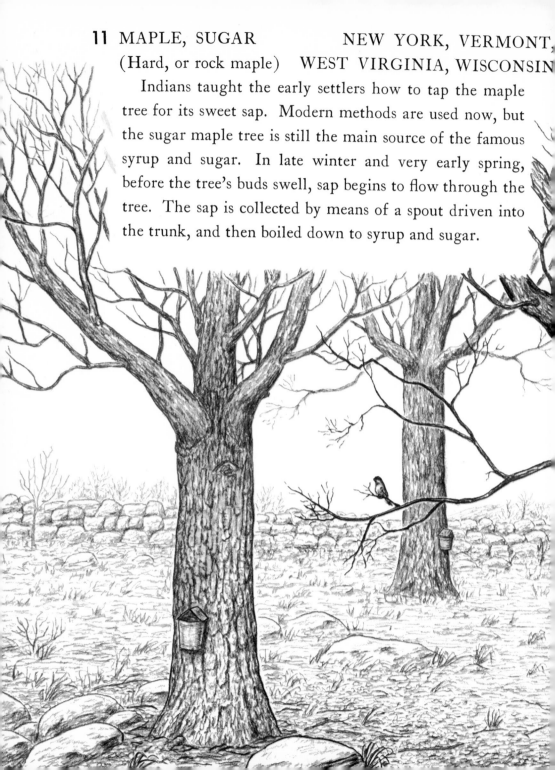

The leaves and flowers of this maple come out at the same time. The pollen and the seed flowers may be on the same tree or on separate ones. Inconspicuous and yellowish in color, they droop from long, slender hairy stems. The yellow-green keys ripen in late summer. The wings, about one inch long, are somewhat larger, and their tips rather more widely spread, than those of the red maple.

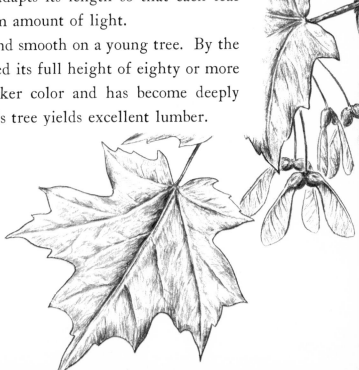

In the typical maple-tree way, the leaves are opposite each other on the twig, and the twigs grow opposite each other on the branch. The leaf, about four inches in width, has five lobes separated by clefts, U-shaped at the base. There are few points on the edges. Each leaf is borne on a long petiole, which adapts its length so that each leaf blade gets the maximum amount of light.

The bark is silvery and smooth on a young tree. By the time the tree has reached its full height of eighty or more feet, the bark is a darker color and has become deeply grooved and flaky. This tree yields excellent lumber.

The live oak is always green, even though it does lose its thick, leathery leaves every year. Each spring they are replaced gradually with bright-green new ones. The flowers also come out at this time. The male catkins hang thickly all over the tree; the small female flowers are

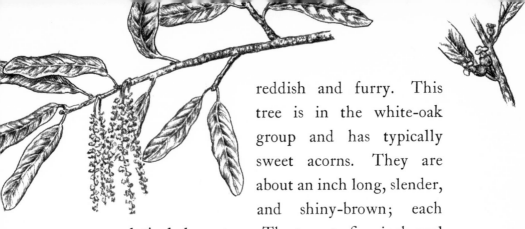

reddish and furry. This tree is in the white-oak group and has typically sweet acorns. They are about an inch long, slender, and shiny-brown; each grows on a relatively long stem. The two- to five-inch oval leaf is not like the general run of oak leaves, for it has no lobes. Dark green and glossy above, it is pale and very hairy beneath.

This tree, which flourishes only in a mild climate, grows rapidly when young. The short gray trunk of an old live oak is greatly enlarged at the base. It divides into massive boughs which, spreading horizontally, form a framework for the domed crown. The tree's width may be greater than its fifty-foot height. Often the branches support a strange rootless plant known as Spanish moss, which collects its food from the air. Sometimes its swaying silvery streamers almost cover the tree.

Whether growing wild in forests or cultivated in parks and gardens, the live oak is at home in sandy soil.

(Bur oak and northern red oak)

The native oak is the official tree of Illinois. Both the northern red oak and the bur (or mossy cup) oak are typical native oaks. The bur oak belongs to the white-oak group; its scientific name means *great-fruited*. The fruit, an acorn, may be two inches long and is a nut set in a deep, broad mossy cup with a hairy fringe at its rim. Often this cup almost covers the sweet-kerneled nut.

The acorns, which mature in one season, develop from small reddish female flowers that perch on a new shoot. The previous year's twigs bear long catkins of yellowish pollen-bearing flowers. Older twigs have corky ridges. The leaves, six to twelve inches long, are the largest of all oak leaves. They vary in shape, but all have irregular rounded lobes. The broad middle part is almost separated from its tapering base by a pair of very deep indentations. The leaf is smooth and dark green on top, but it has a sharply contrasting fuzzy, silvery underside.

This sturdy tree usually has widespread branches and a somewhat fan-shaped crown. Its average height is seventy-five feet, but occasionally it is over one hundred feet tall. The bark of a mature tree is thick, flaky, and deeply ridged, and grayish-brown in color. The tree may live for over two hundred years.

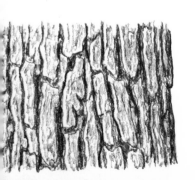

(Common red oak)

The northern red oak belongs to a division of the oaks known as the red-oak group; its members have darker bark than the trees in the white-oak group. They also have bitter instead of sweet acorns, which take two seasons instead of one to mature. And, unlike the leaves of the white oaks, their leaves have veins that run to the end of each bristle-tipped lobe.

The name *red oak* may come from the rich coloring of its autumn foliage and from the pinkish hue of the young leaves. The acorns, twigs, and leafstalks are reddish. Red shows in the furrows of the dark, ridged bark.

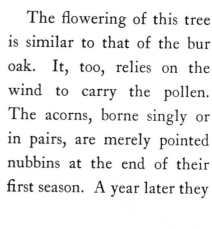

The flowering of this tree is similar to that of the bur oak. It, too, relies on the wind to carry the pollen. The acorns, borne singly or in pairs, are merely pointed nubbins at the end of their first season. A year later they

are stout inch-long acorns,
each set in a shallow, scaly,
saucer-shaped cup.

The smooth leaves are
dark green above and paler
beneath. They are five to eight inches long. As in many
kinds of oaks, they vary greatly in shape and have from
seven to eleven lobes; as a rule, the indentations (known as
sinuses) are not deep.

This tree is the largest of the red-oak group. Ordinarily
it grows to about eighty feet, but is sometimes taller. It
is long-lived and grows rapidly. A mature tree has a thick
trunk, which soon divides into strong boughs. When the
tree grows in the open, its crown is rounded. The hard,
heavy lumber is of great value; it is a favorite material
for floors.

The majestic white oak gives its name to a group of oaks having certain similarities. They have a paler bark than that of the red oaks. Their leaves do not have bristle-tipped lobes. Their acorns are sweet, and mature in one season.

The leaves of the white oak, though always lobed, differ greatly. On the same tree there may be some leaves with shallow notches and others which are cleft almost to the midrib. The limp new leaves are a velvety rose-pink. In the autumn the old ones, which may be as long as nine inches, turn from purple-crimson to rust color. Some may hang on the tree until they are pushed off in the spring by the swelling of the scaled buds.

The catkins of male flowers look yellow because of the stamen's pollen. The tiny pistillate flowers bloom at the base of the new leaves.

About one third (or one quarter inch) of the acorn is covered by a warty cup. When the acorn falls, a gray squirrel may hide it in the earth, if he does not eat it. Then, if he does not dig it up, a stem soon pokes out from its pointed end. This develops a root and a leaf-bearing

shoot. The seedling may
live to be a tree eighty feet
tall, or even taller. And it may live for eight hundred years
as a great tree with a massive trunk and wide-spreading
branches.

The uses of white-oak lumber, which is both beautiful
and durable, are almost numberless.

CANDLENUT (Kukui)

Before the adoption of the candlenut tree (kukui), the coconut palm was the favorite tree of many Hawaiians. This palm has been called man's most valuable tree, for in tropical lands it has provided him with many of his needs—from shelter to food and drink. Perhaps growing to a height of one hundred feet, the tree bears a rosette of leaves at its top; each compound leaf is made up of many two- to three-foot narrow leaflets.

Some of the creamy-white flowers develop into fruit. A mature one has a thick green husk that is the covering of the familiar brown coconut. This shell contains coconut "milk" and "meat." The beginnings of a new tree sprout through the largest of the three scars, or "eyes," seen at the base of the coconut.

The now-favored candlenut tree also was of great importance to the early Hawaiians. Its chief value was in its fruit, a nut that was used as a kind of candle. The kernel of the nut contains an oil that burns brightly. Various methods of using the nut to give light were devised—from

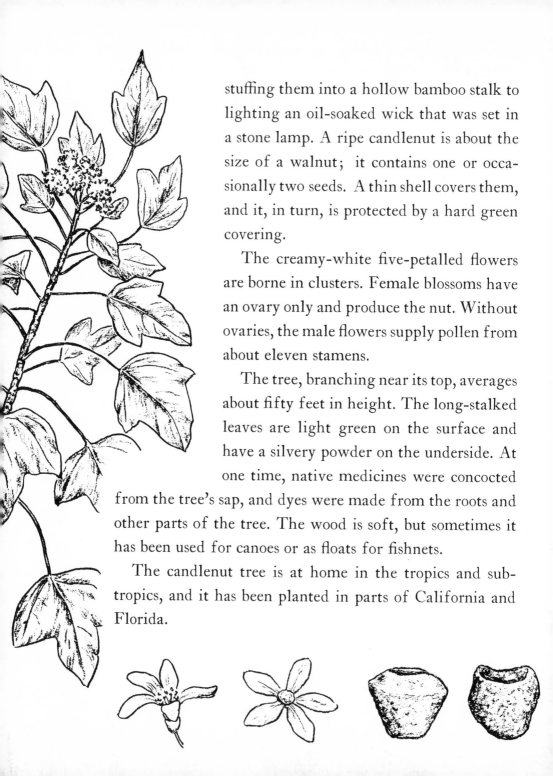

stuffing them into a hollow bamboo stalk to lighting an oil-soaked wick that was set in a stone lamp. A ripe candlenut is about the size of a walnut; it contains one or occasionally two seeds. A thin shell covers them, and it, in turn, is protected by a hard green covering.

The creamy-white five-petalled flowers are borne in clusters. Female blossoms have an ovary only and produce the nut. Without ovaries, the male flowers supply pollen from about eleven stamens.

The tree, branching near its top, averages about fifty feet in height. The long-stalked leaves are light green on the surface and have a silvery powder on the underside. At one time, native medicines were concocted from the tree's sap, and dyes were made from the roots and other parts of the tree. The wood is soft, but sometimes it has been used for canoes or as floats for fishnets.

The candlenut tree is at home in the tropics and subtropics, and it has been planted in parts of California and Florida.

PALMETTO, SABAL

(Sabal palm, cabbage palmetto)

FLORIDA,
SOUTH CAROLINA

The Sabal palmetto belongs to a group of trees known as the fan palms. The giant fan-shaped leaf is divided into many pointed strips. It may be as long as six feet, and its breadth is greater than its length. Long-stalked leaves form an almost round crown at the top of the branchless

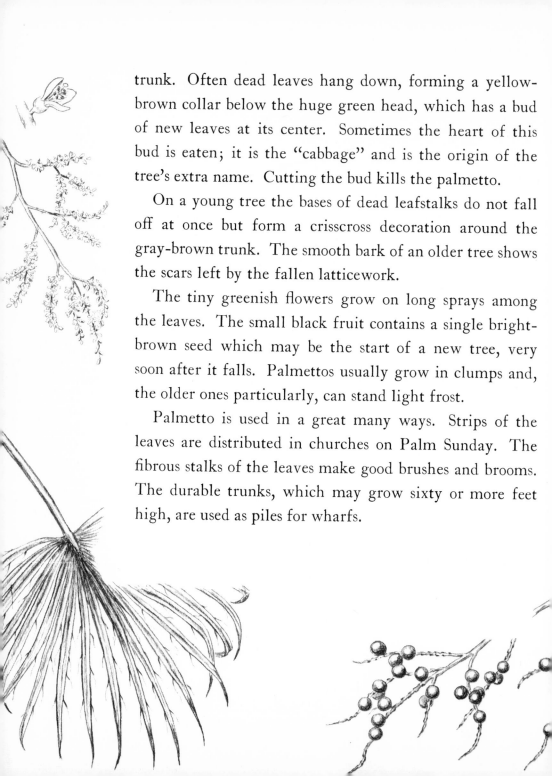

trunk. Often dead leaves hang down, forming a yellow-brown collar below the huge green head, which has a bud of new leaves at its center. Sometimes the heart of this bud is eaten; it is the "cabbage" and is the origin of the tree's extra name. Cutting the bud kills the palmetto.

On a young tree the bases of dead leafstalks do not fall off at once but form a crisscross decoration around the gray-brown trunk. The smooth bark of an older tree shows the scars left by the fallen latticework.

The tiny greenish flowers grow on long sprays among the leaves. The small black fruit contains a single bright-brown seed which may be the start of a new tree, very soon after it falls. Palmettos usually grow in clumps and, the older ones particularly, can stand light frost.

Palmetto is used in a great many ways. Strips of the leaves are distributed in churches on Palm Sunday. The fibrous stalks of the leaves make good brushes and brooms. The durable trunks, which may grow sixty or more feet high, are used as piles for wharfs.

The paloverdes are a small group of strange trees which have leaves only in spring, during the brief rainy season. These leaves fall almost as soon as they are fully grown, which prevents the loss of the tree's moisture by evaporation during the hot, dry summer. The task of making food for the tree, ordinarily the duty of its leaves, is then taken on by the green trunk and the branches. The bark gives the tree its name, for the Spanish words *palo verde* mean *green stick*, or *pole*.

The blue paloverde grows about twenty-five feet tall and has a bluish-green trunk. Its leaves consist of small leaflets on a branched leafstalk. Masses of little flowers cover the tree in early spring. Each has five bright yellow petals and the topmost one is spotted with red. Each stamen's anther—the sac that contains the pollen—is also red. As many as eight seeds may grow in a three- to four-inch pod, which releases them in midsummer.

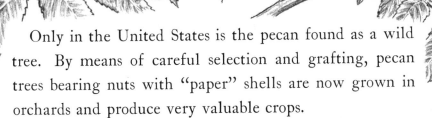

Only in the United States is the pecan found as a wild tree. By means of careful selection and grafting, pecan trees bearing nuts with "paper" shells are now grown in orchards and produce very valuable crops.

Groups of from three to ten nuts develop from tiny female flowers that bloom at the tips of young twigs. Long catkins of male flowers are clustered farther back on the twigs. Each pollinated female flower produces a seed that eventually has a woody shell covered with a thinnish husk. When ripe, and up to two inches long, the husk splits nearly to its base; its four sections open to release a smooth, brown nut, pointed at each end. The empty brown husks may stay on the tree for a long time.

The compound leaves, appearing at the same time as the flowers, have nine to seventeen leaflets along each main

stalk. These narrow leaflets are often curved and have a toothed margin. The whole leaf is twelve to eighteen inches long—the largest leaf found on any member of the hickory clan, to which the pecan belongs.

The pecan flourishes in areas where frost is not too severe and may grow as high as seventy-five feet. Occasionally, in the wilds, it grows very much bigger. A mature pecan tree has an enormous trunk, and its bark is a network of scaled ridges. The widespread lower branches slope downward; the narrow crown is somewhat rounded. Like the wood of other hickories, pecan wood is famous for smoking hams.

(Southern pine, yellow pine, Georgia pine)

The longleaf pine is recognized easily by its eighteen-inch-long needles. When the tree is mature, its tall, straight trunk is topped with twisting branches trimmed with plumes of green. The glossy needles, in groups of three, are enclosed at the base in a silvery sheath. They are shed at the end of their second summer, but the tree is always green, because new leaves have sprouted in the meantime.

The tree begins life in a half-inch-long seed equipped with a long wing. The seeds are shed from a cone, perhaps ten inches long, that has reddish-brown, bristle-tipped scales. It takes two seasons for the cones to ripen, and there is not a good crop every year. They develop from female flowers set at the end of the branch. The short purplish male catkins grow in separate clusters on the same tree.

At first, young seedlings, bearing a fountain of long, flexible needles on a single stem, grow slowly above ground. But below ground they are penetrating the soil very actively, with a long taproot and a mass of rootlets. After a few years, a young pine shoots up very rapidly for a while. At maturity, it reaches a height of about one hundred and twenty feet.

This southern tree is of great service to man. Its strong, durable wood is used in countless ways. Its resin canals are tapped by cutting into the trunk, and the gum which oozes out is collected to produce turpentine and rosin.

(Western yellow pine)

Well over a century ago, an exploring botanist gave this pine its name, because of its ponderous bulk. Its tapering trunk may be eight feet across near the base. Its towering spire of needle-covered branches occasionally soars to a height of more than two hundred feet. A relatively young tree, a mere hundred years old, has dark ridged bark. A five-hundred-year-old tree has cinnamon-red to yellowish bark that is split into oddly shaped brittle segments.

Like other pines, this tree is a conifer, or cone-bearing tree. A young cone stands erect on the branchlet, on its short stalk, until its second year; it turns downward as it matures. Each scale of the three- to six-inch cone has a prickly hook at its thickened tip. Unripe cones are green to plum-purple, but cones ripe enough to open and shed two winged seeds from under each scale are red-brown.

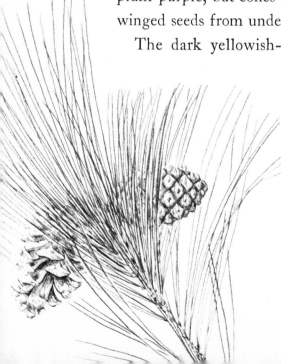

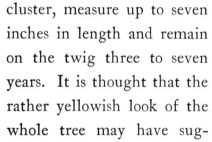

The dark yellowish-green needles, usually three to a cluster, measure up to seven inches in length and remain on the twig three to seven years. It is thought that the rather yellowish look of the whole tree may have sug-

gested the popular name "yellow pine." Features of this pine vary in different parts of its range.

Great forests of these enormous pines provide man with much valuable lumber. To ensure a perpetual supply, seedlings are cared for on tree farms.

(Norway pine)

No one really knows why this native conifer is so often called the Norway pine. The name *red pine* really fits the tree, for the trunk has a flaky reddish bark, and the twig tips and bud scales are reddish-brown. The small female flowers are scarlet. The male ones are purple.

The squat light-brown cones have no prickles. When mature, they are about two inches long. They grow at right angles to the branchlets, which are covered thickly with glossy dark-green needles. The sharply pointed flexible leaves, perhaps as long as six inches, are set in pairs enclosed in a papery sheath at the base. They live for four or five years. The straight trunk is usually sixty to eighty feet tall. It has branches in whorls; that is, they grow from the trunk like spokes from the hub of a wheel.

Red pine is in demand for building log cabins, as well as for general construction work.

(Yellow pine)

This pine's botanical name means *hedgehog*, and it describes the small egg-shaped cone, which has a short, nearly straight spine on every scale. The points are soon shed. The cones ripen in two seasons and then open, freeing light winged seeds that may be blown far from the parent tree. Often empty cones stay on the tree for a few years.

The tree may grow to about one hundred feet. Having shed its lower branches as it matured, it has a straight trunk topped with an open crown. The bark has large, irregularly oblong scales of a reddish or grayish color. If the trunk is destroyed, this pine has the ability, unique among pines, to sprout new growth from its root.

The dark-green needles, three to five inches long, grow in twos, though occasionally three slender, flexible leaves are found growing together. The yellowish wood is strong and stiff; it is used widely for house building.

The eastern white pine has an honored place in history, for it served the early settlers well. The tall branchless trunks were in great demand for the masts of sailing ships and were exported far and wide. The finest trees were marked by the king's surveyors for use by the Royal Navy. Some trees are said to have been two hundred and fifty feet tall in those days. There are none so tall now, but this tree is still the tallest conifer in the East.

The branches, growing in whorls, usually are in circles of five. Each whorl marks a year's growth for the tree. The young tree is shaped like a pyramid and grows rapidly for a time. An old tree has a straight trunk, dark-gray furrowed bark, and a narrow, irregular crown.

The bright pinkish-purple female flowers grow on the upper part of the tree and normally come out in June. The stamen-bearing flowers appear on the new shoots of the lower branches, releasing yellow clouds of pollen in the wind, or when a branch is touched.

The tree's erect young cones are about an inch long at the end of their first season. As they grow longer and heavier, they droop.

After turning from green to brown, each cone, now about eight inches long, is ripe. There are two winged seeds under each scale.

The blue-green needles, from three to five inches long, and in bunches of five, form soft plumes at each twig's end. The yellow-green needles that appeared in the spring are bright against the dark, older ones, which do not fall for two or three years.

(Mountain pine, silver pine, finger-cone pine)

This western brother of the eastern white pine comes naturally by its other names. White-pine forests grow up mountainsides, but its ability to thrive at high altitudes does not bar this tree from flourishing at sea level as well. It is also known as silver pine, because the bark of a young tree is silvery. On older trees, though, the squarish blocks of bark are grayish-purple to reddish-brown. The tree grows to a height of one hundred and fifty feet and may live for five hundred years.

The needles, which grow in bunches of five, are shorter, stiffer, and more thickly set than those of the eastern white pine. And the long-stalked cones are longer and slimmer. Often growing in clusters, they are the finger cones that give the tree one of its names.

This is a timber tree of many uses—from matchsticks to building construction.

(Common nut pine)

The botanist's name for this pine, which is an important source of food, means *edible*. Indians in its area, after removing the thin shell, prepare the seed, or nut, in many ways. Two plump wingless seeds are borne under each thick scale of the globular or egg-shaped cone.

This tree grows slowly, but it thrives in spite of drought, frost, and extreme heat. It may produce crops of nuts for over three hundred years. Its short needles help it to survive, because a needle-shaped leaf does not lose so much water by evaporation as a broad leaf does. The stiff needles, averaging an inch in length, usually grow in twos but occasionally in threes. This bushy, spreading pine some-

times reaches a height of forty feet. It has a broad trunk with a grayish or reddish-brown bark.

In identifying pines, the number of needles in a cluster is an important clue. The one-leaf piñon is the only pine whose needles grow singly. However, needles in pairs are not unknown. The needles are sharp-pointed, about two inches long, and somewhat curved. Their green color has a whitish tinge.

This tree has a short trunk and its limbs are gnarled like those of an old apple tree. It is usually about twenty feet in height but often grows taller. It is very hardy and can grow on arid mountains.

The seeds, or nuts, are a valuable food. They grow as long as three quarters of an inch, under the scales of a roundish or oval cone about three and a half inches long.

The wood is used for firewood. It makes excellent charcoal which is in great demand.

(Tacamahac)

The branches of this cottonwood, or balsam poplar, form a rather narrow oval crown. The tapered leaf has a round leafstalk, so the blade does not flutter perpetually like the leaves of some poplars or cottonwoods.

This tree is famous for its large winter buds, which are fragrant and sticky. In the spring, bees collect the softened gum, or resin, from the buds and use it as a cement, called propolis, to seal cracks in their hives. This resin is sometimes used in cough syrup.

The balsam poplar likes moist, even wet, soil. It grows happily along stream beds and is common in prairie country. Often it is planted as a windbreak, or cultivated as a shade tree near homes and along streets.

Like the eastern cottonwood, the balsam poplar bears male and female flower catkins on separate trees.

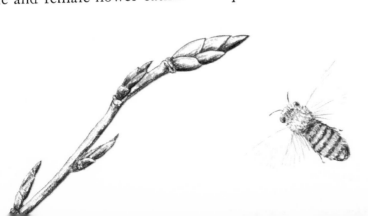

(Necklace poplar)

This tree, the largest member of the cottonwood family, is often called the necklace poplar. Children make necklaces from the seed pods which hang from the tree on strings from six to eleven inches long. When ripe, the seed pods split and let loose masses of white fluff containing minute seeds. This "cotton" grows only from the flowers of female trees. The male tree bears many catkins, or ropes, of flowers with showy red stamens. They shed their pollen quickly and fall, looking like fat crimson caterpillars asleep beneath the tree.

This poplar's toothed triangular leaves come

out later than the flowers. The leaf is broad and its long leafstalk, or petiole, is flattened sideways so that it is caught by the slightest breeze. The whole tree rustles continuously.

A mature tree has a broad open crown and is about one hundred feet tall, though an occasional specimen may reach one hundred and fifty feet. It grows very fast but is usually short-lived. Because of its very wide-spreading roots, it is able to thrive in poor soil better than any other tree and can stand extreme heat, cold, and drought.

(Judas tree)

The tiny buds of the redbud are red in winter, but it is not till early spring that this native tree really shows up among the bare trees around it. Before its own leaves are out, thousands of little magenta flowers spring, in clusters, from the naked twigs, the main branches, and even from the trunk. The flower is like a pea blossom, and the seeds develop in a flattened pod that turns purple as it ripens. The two- to four-inch-long pods are hidden by shiny heart-shaped leaves, perhaps six inches long, which unfold as the flowers fade.

The tree has a short trunk which branches to form a roundish head. Depending on its location, it grows to heights varying from ten to fifty feet.

The redbud is also known as the Judas tree because, according to legend, Judas hanged himself on a tree of the same family, whose white flowers turned red with shame.

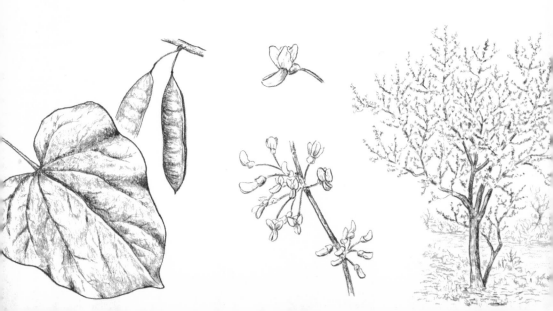

(Coast redwood and giant sequoia or big tree)

The coastal tree and its Sierra relative, the big tree, have the same botanical name, *sequoia*, in honor of the Cherokee chief, Sequoya, who devised an alphabet for his tribe.

Though not the oldest tree known, the coast redwood is the tallest. Living for two thousand years and often reaching three hundred and fifty feet in height, this huge evergreen conifer grows from a seed one sixteenth of an inch across—or about the size of the letter *o* on this page.

Four or five wing-bordered seeds lie under each scale of

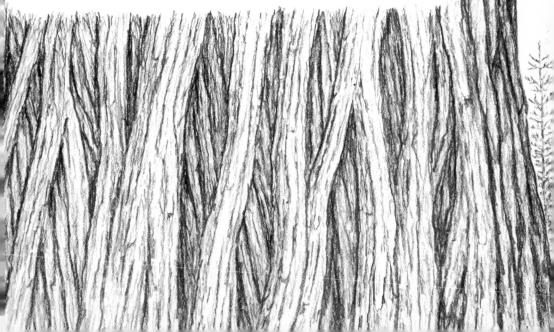

a tiny cone which is often less than an inch long. The cones ripen in one season and hang on the tree for some months after shedding their seeds. Many of the seeds are imperfect, but some of them may grow. The forests are also replenished by the sprouting of tree stumps.

This towering tree's small leaves take two forms. On the lower branches they grow on the opposite sides of a twig in a flat spray. On the higher branches the leaves, only one quarter of an inch long, are similar in form to those on the big tree.

The mighty trunk of the coast redwood is red, tinged with gray. Its thick bark is so deeply and widely furrowed that a person can stand between the ridges. The straight column of a maturing tree rises to a great height before its branches form the tree's relatively narrow crown. Young trees are green to the base.

This redwood needs heavy rains and the moisture of sea fogs in order to thrive.

The giant sequoia, or big tree, dwarfs the tallest fir trees near it. It is not so sky-piercing as the coast redwood, but its greater girth and massive branches make it a mightier tree. Its age is greater too; some big trees are estimated to have lived for five thousand years. The buttressed cinnamon-red trunk of one famous giant has so broad a base that it can barely be encircled by twenty men with their arms outstretched.

This tree needs an efficient root system to supply water

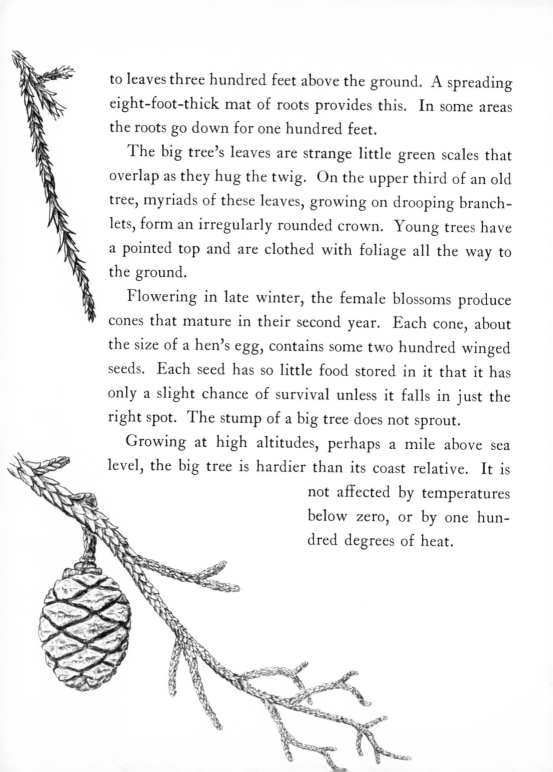

to leaves three hundred feet above the ground. A spreading eight-foot-thick mat of roots provides this. In some areas the roots go down for one hundred feet.

The big tree's leaves are strange little green scales that overlap as they hug the twig. On the upper third of an old tree, myriads of these leaves, growing on drooping branchlets, form an irregularly rounded crown. Young trees have a pointed top and are clothed with foliage all the way to the ground.

Flowering in late winter, the female blossoms produce cones that mature in their second year. Each cone, about the size of a hen's egg, contains some two hundred winged seeds. Each seed has so little food stored in it that it has only a slight chance of survival unless it falls in just the right spot. The stump of a big tree does not sprout.

Growing at high altitudes, perhaps a mile above sea level, the big tree is hardier than its coast relative. It is not affected by temperatures below zero, or by one hundred degrees of heat.

Black Hills spruce is a variety of the white spruce. It has a limited range and seems to be at home only in parts of South Dakota. Its needles are a brighter green and grow more densely than those of the faster-growing white spruce.

Like other spruces, this tree seldom bears cones on its lower branches. The oval cones, up to one and a half inches long, hang in profusion on the upper part of the pointed tree. The inch-long needles, growing singly around the twig, are notorious for their unpleasant odor when bruised. The white spruce, which is similar, is nicknamed "skunk spruce." because of this smell. These trees are famous for their wood, which is used extensively for paper pulp.

(Colorado spruce)

This tree is often seen far from its native Rocky Mountain forests. Young spruce trees—compact, silvery-blue
pyramids that grow slowly—are planted in the parks and
gardens of many states. The trunks of such trees may be
hidden by closely set whorls of needled branches. Old
trees, with furrowed bark, are likely to be less shapely.

The stiff curved needles, about one inch long, have a
horny pointed tip and are four-sided. They bristle from
all around the branchlets, each one set on a tiny stub which
remains after the leaf has fallen. Old leaves are a dull
green.

The male flowers form a cone-shaped catkin in the angle
between leaf and twig. The female flowers grow on the
same tree, at the end of the twig. The ripened tan-colored
cone, two to four inches long, hangs downward; each of
its thin, tapering scales has a jagged tip. The cone opens
at the end of its first season to shed its winged seeds, which
are only about an eighth of

an inch long. Empty cones may hang on the tree through the winter.

Usually eighty to one hundred feet high, an exceptional blue spruce may be a hundred and fifty feet.

(Yellow poplar, tulip poplar)

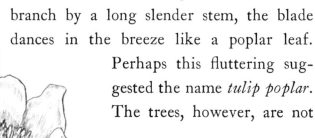

Even during its winter rest, the tulip tree is striking. When the golden-yellow autumn leaves fall, the three-inch-long fruit cones, tan in color, still point skyward. Most of the seeds on the upper part of the cone's central spike are soon whirled away, but the seeds on the lower section, with their inch-long wings, remain. In winter, they look like fringed flowers on the bare tree.

The real flowers, which are shaped like a tulip and give the tree its name, bloom among the leaves in early summer. Six greenish-yellow petals, each splashed with an orange band, form a cup about two inches deep. Below it, three creamy sepals point downward. Inside, a ring of long stamens surround a tightly grouped collection of pistils which develop into the seed cone.

The glossy leaves are unlike any others. Usually four-lobed, and with a peculiar squarish tip, the four- to six-inch leaf blade is as broad as it is long. Attached to the branch by a long slender stem, the blade dances in the breeze like a poplar leaf. Perhaps this fluttering suggested the name *tulip poplar*. The trees, however, are not

in the same family. The yellow wood of the tulip tree, like that of the poplar, is easily worked.

The large purplish winter buds are unusual. Two leaf-like scales form a flattish packet which contains more and more packets, one inside the other. Under each layer a perfect miniature leaf is folded down. In the spring the coverings fall away as the shoot within grows and the new young leaves straighten up their bent-over blades.

Commonly the tulip tree grows to about eighty feet, but in woodlands it may be almost two hundred feet tall. As with other kinds of trees, the description of the shape of one tulip tree does not apply to all. A tulip tree, crowded by other trees, may grow for a hundred feet before branching. In the open, the lower limbs, growing from a divided trunk, may turn downward to sweep the ground. The bark, which was smooth in youth, is grooved with interlaced furrows in age. In many kinds of trees the pattern of the outer bark alters because of the pressure of the growing wood beneath it.

CYPRESS, BALD LOUISIANA Unlike its evergreen relatives, this cypress sheds its narrow, half-inch-long leaves every autumn; they are arranged spirally on the twigs. About one inch across, the purplish, seed-bearing cones are almost round. The tree is famous for its "knees," which project from the roots and rise above the swamp water or mud to a height of several feet. These hollow "knees" are thought to provide air for the roots of the tree.

PINE, LOBLOLLY NORTH CAROLINA Occasionally reaching a height of one hundred and seventy feet, this pine has a straight trunk with a deeply grooved bark. The somewhat egg-shaped cones take two seasons to mature; then they are up to six inches long. The leaves are sharply pointed needles, five to nine inches in length; they are borne in sets of three and are held together by a sheath at the base.

SPRUCE, SITKA ALASKA This spruce is the tallest North American spruce and may grow to a height of over two hundred feet. The flat, prickly needles sprout straight out all around the twigs. The flexible cones hang from the ends of branches and are two to four inches long. The Sitka spruce is an important lumber tree.

WALNUT, BLACK IOWA Possibly this walnut is designated black because of the dark color of the deeply ridged shell that contains the edible kernel. It develops inside a thick, green husk. The nuts are produced by female flowers. The pollen-bearing male flowers grow on a hanging stem. The compound leaves have up to twenty-three leaflets.